THE WIRE BENDING BOOK

INTERSTELLAR

TRADING & PUBLISHING COMPANY

LA MESA, CALIFORNIA

ISBN 0-9645957-9-6
LIBRARY OF CONGRESS CATALOG NUMBER: 97-93597
SAN: 298-5829

Illustrations by Wendy Simpson Conner
Color Photography by Don Brandos
Printed in the United States of America

FIRST PRINTING: DECEMBER, 1998

ACKNOWLEDGMENTS:
To Jennie, Priscilla, Joni, Paul and Mel;
and everyone who bought and loved
THE BEST LITTLE BEADING BOOK,
THE BEADED LAMPSHADE BOOK,
THE MAGICAL BEADED MEDICINE BAG BOOK.
THE 'KNOTTY' MACRAME AND BEADING BOOK
THE BEADED WATCHBAND BOOK
THE CHAIN & CRYSTAL BOOK
THE BEADED JEWELRY FOR A WEDDING BOOK
THE CHILDREN'S BEADING BOOK
THE CAT LOVER'S BEADED PROJECT BOOK

INTRODUCTION

When I was about ten years old we went to Mexico. There was a man on the streets who had a cart filled with wire. For one dollar, he would twist this wire and make a pin with the letters of your name. I was fascinated as I watched his fingers fly; the pliers and his hand were as one. And when he finished, here was this beautiful pin with absolutely perfect penmanship, spelling "Wendy" in multiple strands of wire.

Every year we would go to the Del Mar Fair. There were people there who would create things out of wire. People would challenge them, "Make a horse," or "Make a car," and they would do just that. I was always reminded of those guys who make the balloon animals. They seemed so sure with their movements; such perfection in motion.

After these trips to the fair, I used to dream about wire and thread shooting from the tips of my fingers. Like a human spider, I would spin jewelry in my sleep.

Wire is one of the hottest looks right now. A woman I know showed me a beautiful wire-wrapped pendant she bought at a gemshow. She paid over $100 for it. It was lovely, but in all honesty, there was only about $10 in materials used. The appreciation is definitely in the artistry.

Wire is an addictive medium. As you complete each project, you will think, "How would it look if I did this or that next time?"

There is a wide variety of wire projects in this book; wire wrapping, making coils and spirals, using a jig, Peruvian-style wirework, knitting with wire, and a lot more.

I hope you enjoy this book. This is part of a series of 25 books called **The Beading Books Series.** Other books in the series include *The Best Little Beading Book, The Beaded Lampshade Book, The Magical Beaded Medicine Bag Book, The "Knotty" Macrame and Beading Book, The Beaded Watchband Book, The Chain & Crystal Book, The Beaded Jewelry for a Wedding Book, The Children's Beading Book,* and *The Cat Lover's Beaded Project Book.*

As always, I love hearing your wonderful comments. Please feel free to write to me c/o The Interstellar Trading and Publishing Company, Post Office Box 2215, La Mesa, CA 91943. *HAPPY BEADING!*™

"Me"

TABLE OF CONTENTS

TYPES OF WIRE

There are so many types of wire, that you can use different wires on your projects, and each look will be distinct. Wires have different properties. Some hold their shape well, some are soft and lose their structure quickly.

Sizes and Shapes

Wire comes in gauges (determining thickness). The higher the number, the thinner the wire (a #32 is thinner and generally weaker than a #24). Among wire gauges are #14, #16, #18, #20, #22, #24, #26, #28, #32. A #14 requires good pliers and lots of stamina (it's stiff and not as easy to manipulate). If you are going to weave or knit wire, the thinner ones (#24 on up) are easier. Generally, earwires and headpins are #22 or #24. Most drilled beads fit easily on this size.

Wire has different strengths, too. Hard, half hard and soft are available.

Wire also comes in shapes. You usually think of it being round, but there is also flat, half round, and square. You can use flat wire for wrapping, square wire for twisting and bending, and half round for caging stones. There are no set rules, using a variety adds depth to your work.

Precious Metal Wire

Gold filled and sterling wires are beautiful to work with. 24k gold wire is also available, but not recommended. It's pricey and weak, and dents very easily.. The higher the level of gold, the weaker the wire. Gold filled gives the prestige of gold without the pitfalls.

Sterling is wonderful (my personal favorite). You can actually make your own. It's a painstaking process to draw your own wire, but it is very gratifying. You can work with sterling in its natural state, or apply a patina to give an antique look.

Jeweler's Wire

This is what you find in craft and bead stores. It comes on spools, and is available in several colors, including gold, silver, copper, green, red, and black.

Other Wires

I admit it: I am a telephone wire junkie. Whenever I can, I acquire the wire that is used for telephones, strip the conduit, and work with the wire. It is bundled in coordinating colors (how nice of them to do this); striped blue with solid blue, striped brown with solid brown, etc. You can create some pretty unusual jewelry.

Titanium is another beautiful wire to work with. The deep purple color is gorgeous and rich.

The only caution is if you find a wire and you're not sure of its metal content, you may want to test it before you make a bazillion projects out of it. You wouldn't want to make earrings that create an infection, or bracelets that turn arms green!

Having the right plier or needle is like a painter having the right brush. It makes your work so much easier! The wrong plier can mar your wire, and make dents that are visible.

The more pliers and tools you have, the greater the variety of effects you can achieve.

It is even helpful to have multiples of certain pliers, like the CHAIN NOSE or DUCKBILL. This way you can grip with greater ease. Test your pliers on a scrap of wire before you begin a project. When shifting from a harder wire to a softer one, the same pliers may work for one but not the other.

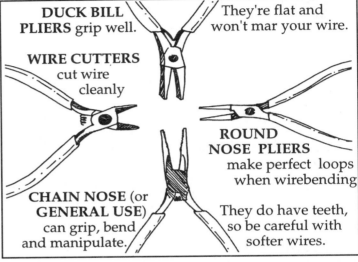

DUCK BILL PLIERS grip well. They're flat and won't mar your wire.

WIRE CUTTERS cut wire cleanly

ROUND NOSE PLIERS make perfect loops when wirebending

CHAIN NOSE (or GENERAL USE) can grip, bend and manipulate.

They do have teeth, so be careful with softer wires.

A WIRE JIG is a device that you can make yourself by driving nails into a block of wood. You can use graph paper to map out designs, arrange your nails in your pattern, and wrap your wire around the nails for repeatable, matched components.

A HELPING HAND is a device that holds items in place so that they can be soldered without burning your hand. It's useful for gripping.

A SOLDERING GUN secures wire into place for strength. Be sure to use the right kind of solder for your wire: gold, silver, lead, etc.

NEEDLE FILES smooth rough edges, and are great for sharpening pin points.

PATINAS are useful for coloring and oxidizing your wires. These are available from paint stores.

These are just some of the techniques that can be used with wire.

Simple Loops

Using your round nose pliers, make a loop in the wire. Try to use a smooth rolling motion. Roll the wire over the end of the plier.
The size of the loop will depend on how much wire is in your loop (generally, 1/2" per loop is plenty), and how close you are to the tip of the plier.

Vertical Coils

Use two chain nose pliers to grip and coil the ends.

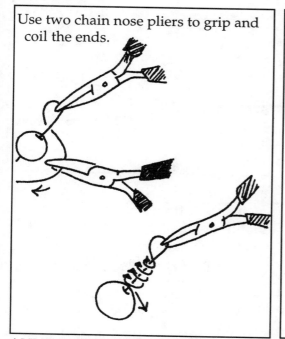

Horizontal Coils

Work your plier and wire in a circular motion.

Start with a small bend or circle in your wire.

Continuing in the same direction as the first bend, grip with your plier and smoothly fill out the coil.

ANNEALING WIRE is when you use a heat source, you can soften your wire for easier working. You may want to experiment with how your wire's characteristics change with temperature.

Making Jumprings

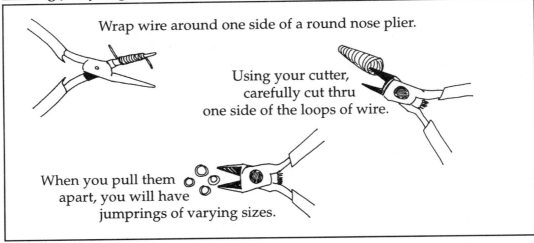

Wrap wire around one side of a round nose plier.

Using your cutter, carefully cut thru one side of the loops of wire.

When you pull them apart, you will have jumprings of varying sizes.

Twisting Wire

There are two very easy ways to twist wire.

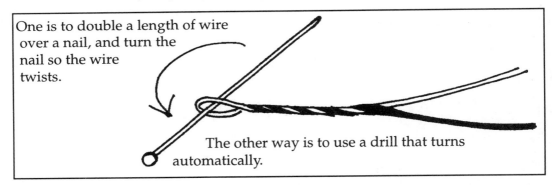

One is to double a length of wire over a nail, and turn the nail so the wire twists.

The other way is to use a drill that turns automatically.

Wire Applique

You can wirebend silver wire into a design, then solder it onto a sheet of silver.

This is great for earrings and brooches.

Wire Wraps

For an usual effect, wrap one wire around another. This looks great when they are different colors. You can also use these wrapped pieces as beads.

The Wire Bending Book

This style of wire bending is very easy, yet looks so impressive.

Using the wrapping technique shown on page 8, wrap a long length of wire (1-2 feet). Use a heavier gauge for your core (appx. #18) than for your wrap wire.

Once you have wrapped a long enough length, start a vertical coiling motion as shown on page 7.

Start with a loop at the top and end with a loop at the bottom.

Work tightly. Continue until you have made a bead.

For a nice variation, try coiling your core wire at the top and bottom of the bead.

You can also interweave unwrapped wires like your core wire or a wire of another color with the wrapped wires.

You can make any finding with wire!

Earwires:

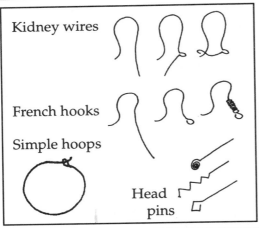

Kidney wires

French hooks

Simple hoops

Head pins

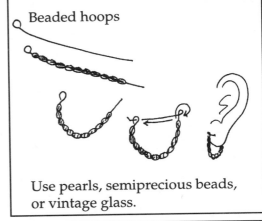

Beaded hoops

Use pearls, semiprecious beads, or vintage glass.

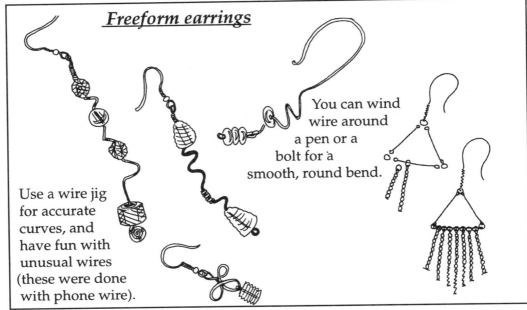

Freeform earrings

Use a wire jig for accurate curves, and have fun with unusual wires (these were done with phone wire).

You can wind wire around a pen or a bolt for a smooth, round bend.

Sterling Clasp:

Using the techniques shown on pages 7 and 9, take a length of #14 gauge wire and embellish with a piece of #20 wire that has been coiled in the center with #24 wire. The embellished section should be about 1/2 to 3/4" wide.

Bend the ends to make hooks.

Attach with jumprings.

Hook and Eye Clasp: Leather Pendant Necklace

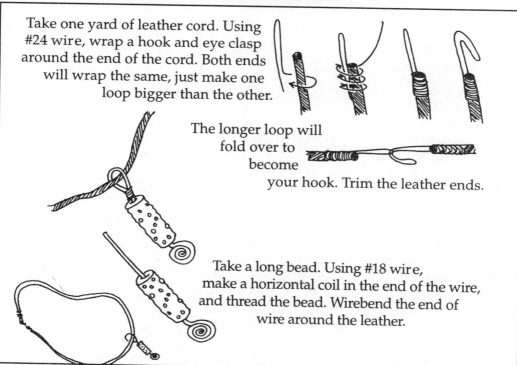

Take one yard of leather cord. Using #24 wire, wrap a hook and eye clasp around the end of the cord. Both ends will wrap the same, just make one loop bigger than the other.

The longer loop will fold over to become your hook. Trim the leather ends.

Take a long bead. Using #18 wire, make a horizontal coil in the end of the wire, and thread the bead. Wirebend the end of wire around the leather.

COLOR PHOTO INDEX

some of the projects included in this book are not shown in full color

Simple Seedbead Ring

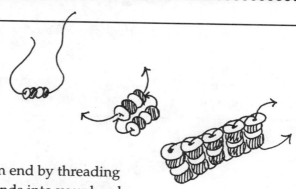

Take a one foot length of #28 gauge wire and add 4 9/0 seedbeads. Center the beads on the wire, and criss cross through the seedbeads.

Work to length, then end by threading the ends into your beads.

Bent Wire Ring

MATERIALS:

- #18 and #24 gauge wir es   - Assortment of beads   - Two chain nose pliers
- Wire cutters - A wooden 3/4" dowel

Cut a 2" piece of 18 gauge wire and wrap it loosely around a 3/4" dowel. This will make the main curve for your ring. You can adjust for sizing. Using your pliers, bend the wire to form a small loop at one end. Cut the wire to fit 3/4 of the way around your finger, then bend the second end into a small loop. Be sure the loops are parallel to the plane of the ring.

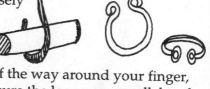

Thread your beads onto a length of #24 wir e. Wrap the end smoothly through the loop of the #18, and coil car efully. Thread the other end of the wire through the other loop of the #18, and coil tightly to match the other side.

Use this ring sizer to help measure your wire.

5 6 7 8 9 10

Threading beads on jumprings makes a very different look.

MATERIALS:
- 90 4mm rose quartz beads
- 15 1/2" jumprings (make them with #22 or #24 wir e)
- Two chain nose pliers and one wire cutter
- 15" in chain

Cut your chain into 1" pieces.
Use a chain with a link that
accommodates your rings.

Thread the chain
onto a jumpring.
Add one rose quartz
bead to each
side of the chain.
Close the jumpring.
If using sterling,
you may choose to
solder them shut.

Add two more jumprings with rose quartz beads, and interlink
all three jumprings together.

Join the units together.
When you are done, you will
have a continuous necklace long enough
to go over your head without a clasp.

SIMPLE LINKED NECKLACE

This very basic necklace is easy to make.

MATERIALS:

- 45 garnet 4mm beads
- #24 sterling wire
- One sterling lobster claw clasp

- Round nose plier
- Wire cutter
- Chain nose plier

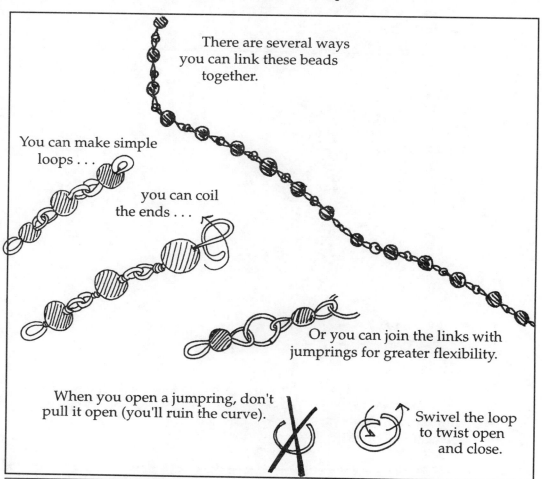

There are several ways you can link these beads together.

You can make simple loops . . .

you can coil the ends . . .

Or you can join the links with jumprings for greater flexibility.

When you open a jumpring, don't pull it open (you'll ruin the curve).

Swivel the loop to twist open and close.

Using the same techniques as the Simple Linked Necklace from the previous page, you can add heishi beads (flat metal disks) to change the look.

MATERIALS:
- #22 sterling wire
- Brass heishi beads
- An assortment of vintage glass and crystal beads in amethyst, amber, vitrial, and clear.
- Chain nose pliers
- Wire cutters

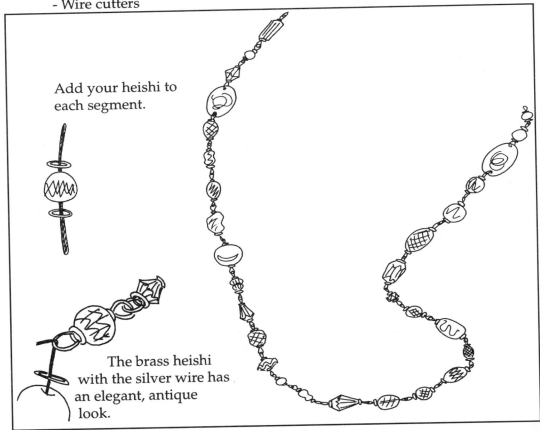

Add your heishi to each segment.

The brass heishi with the silver wire has an elegant, antique look.

Handmade Rosaries make a very personal gift. You can make rosaries out of crystal, birthstones, beads that have been in the family for years . . . almost any type of bead will do.

MATERIALS NEEDED:
- Fifty beads of one type (main bead)
- Nine beads that are similiar or different (spacer beads)
- #20 or #22 gauge wir e
- One crucifix
- One Rosary centerpiece
- Sixteen jumprings
- Your pliers

The pattern is 10 main beads, one jump ring, one spacer bead, one jump ring, 10 main beads, one jump ring, one spacer bead, one jump ring, 10 main beads, one jump ring, one spacer bead, one jump ring, 10 main beads, one jump ring, one spacer bead, one jump ring, 10 main beads. Be sure that it begins and ends with the 10 main beads.

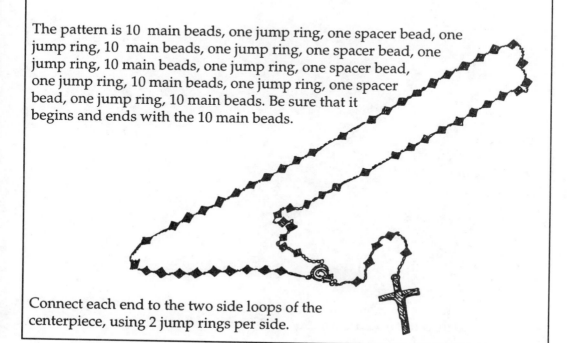

Connect each end to the two side loops of the centerpiece, using 2 jump rings per side.

You can use this link in your rosary, or in the necklace shown here.

MATERIALS:
- Flat silver wire(appx. 3 yds)
- #22 silver wire (about 1 ft)
- Round nose pliers   - Chain nose pliers   - Wire cutters

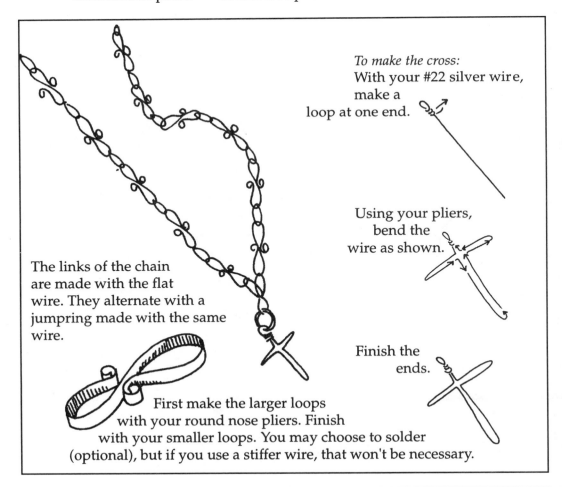

To make the cross:
With your #22 silver wire, make a loop at one end.

Using your pliers, bend the wire as shown.

Finish the ends.

The links of the chain are made with the flat wire. They alternate with a jumpring made with the same wire.

First make the larger loops with your round nose pliers. Finish with your smaller loops. You may choose to solder (optional), but if you use a stiffer wire, that won't be necessary.

Suncatchers make wonderful gifts.

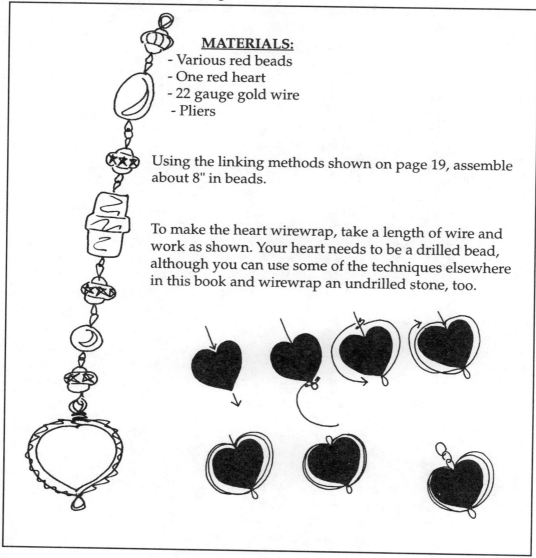

MATERIALS:
- Various red beads
- One red heart
- 22 gauge gold wire
- Pliers

Using the linking methods shown on page 19, assemble about 8" in beads.

To make the heart wirewrap, take a length of wire and work as shown. Your heart needs to be a drilled bead, although you can use some of the techniques elsewhere in this book and wirewrap an undrilled stone, too.

This suncatcher is made with a "liquid glass", which is a plastic-like substance that looks like glass. It's used for painted projects that resemble stained glass.

MATERIALS:
- Two teal 12mm crystal beads
- Three 6mm fuschia crystals
- 22 gauge silver wire (doesn't need to be sterling)
- Pliers
- Five jumprings
- Two bottle of "liquid glass": one in teal and one in fuschia

Design your dragonfly and bend your wire, using a combination of pliers and your wirejig (if you trace the graphed design, and lay it on the wirejig, put your nails at the points shown. You can then manipulate as needed to get your finished design. The dragonfly shown is smaller than the finished piece.

Lay your wire dragonfly on waxed paper. Carefully fill the open wire loops with the "liquid glass". Let dry completely, and attach.

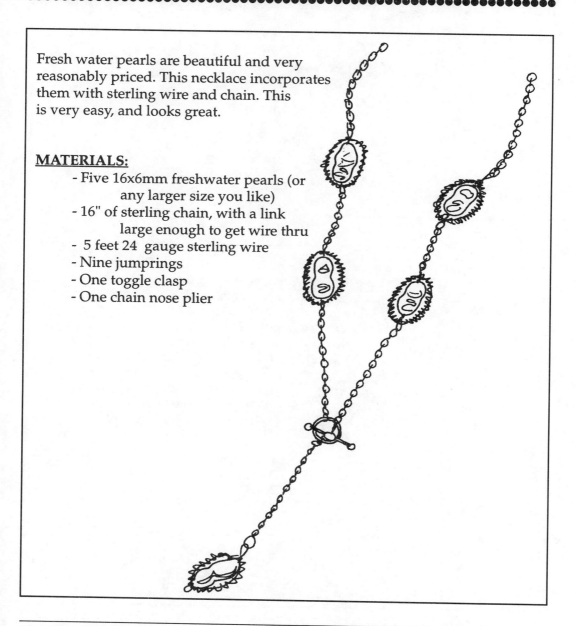

Fresh water pearls are beautiful and very reasonably priced. This necklace incorporates them with sterling wire and chain. This is very easy, and looks great.

MATERIALS:

- Five 16x6mm freshwater pearls (or any larger size you like)
- 16" of sterling chain, with a link large enough to get wire thru
- 5 feet 24 gauge sterling wire
- Nine jumprings
- One toggle clasp
- One chain nose plier

STEP ONE:

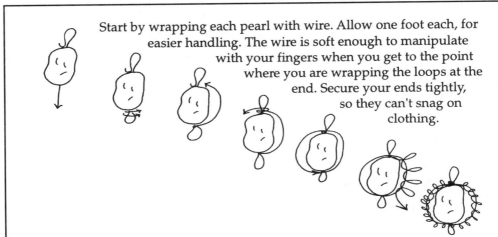

Start by wrapping each pearl with wire. Allow one foot each, for easier handling. The wire is soft enough to manipulate with your fingers when you get to the point where you are wrapping the loops at the end. Secure your ends tightly, so they can't snag on clothing.

STEP TWO:

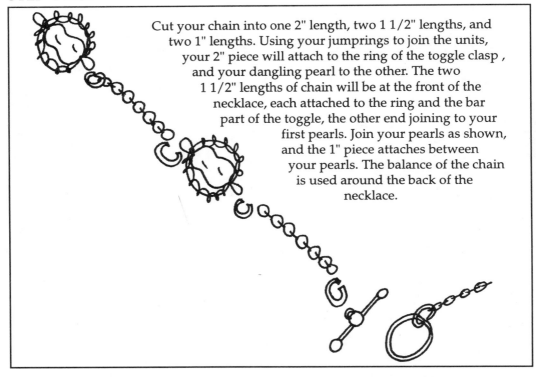

Cut your chain into one 2" length, two 1 1/2" lengths, and two 1" lengths. Using your jumprings to join the units, your 2" piece will attach to the ring of the toggle clasp , and your dangling pearl to the other. The two 1 1/2" lengths of chain will be at the front of the necklace, each attached to the ring and the bar part of the toggle, the other end joining to your first pearls. Join your pearls as shown, and the 1" piece attaches between your pearls. The balance of the chain is used around the back of the necklace.

The Wire Bending Book

Chandelier crystals are easy to find at flea markets. They are usually flat, with sideways holes in the top and bottom, but they are not drilled like a bead. I hoarded these blue ones until I found the perfect project for them.

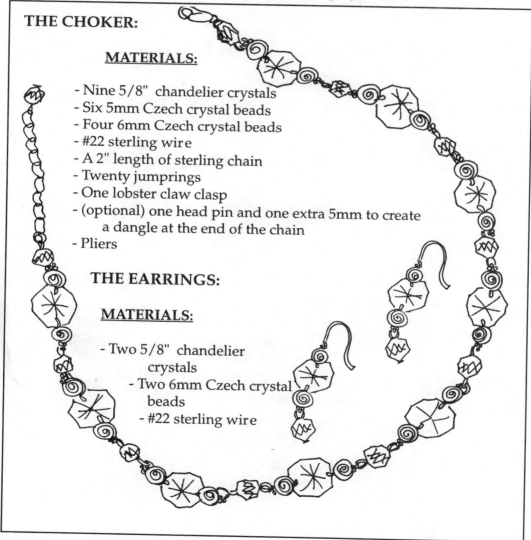

THE CHOKER:

MATERIALS:

- Nine 5/8" chandelier crystals
- Six 5mm Czech crystal beads
- Four 6mm Czech crystal beads
- #22 sterling wire
- A 2" length of sterling chain
- Twenty jumprings
- One lobster claw clasp
- (optional) one head pin and one extra 5mm to create a dangle at the end of the chain
- Pliers

THE EARRINGS:

MATERIALS:

- Two 5/8" chandelier crystals
- Two 6mm Czech crystal beads
- #22 sterling wire

STEP ONE:

Make a coil in a length of wire.

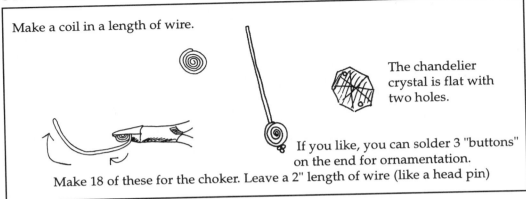

The chandelier crystal is flat with two holes.

If you like, you can solder 3 "buttons" on the end for ornamentation.

Make 18 of these for the choker. Leave a 2" length of wire (like a head pin)

STEP TWO:

Loop the shaft of the spiraled pin through one of the holes in your crystal.

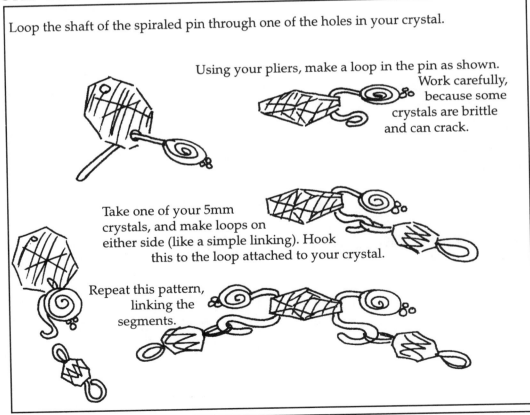

Using your pliers, make a loop in the pin as shown. Work carefully, because some crystals are brittle and can crack.

Take one of your 5mm crystals, and make loops on either side (like a simple linking). Hook this to the loop attached to your crystal.

Repeat this pattern, linking the segments.

STEP THREE:

As you work, remember to put your largest crystal (the 6mm at the center of the choker. The smaller (5mm crystal) is on the outer ends.

When your are done, end with a linked 5mm crystal. Using jumprings, attach to your clasp and chain.

Add a dangle to the end of the chain if you like. Make the dangle with a 5mm crystal on a head pin, and attach to the end of the chain

THE EARRINGS:

Using the same linking design as the choker, Make an earwire out of one of your pins. Be sure to allow for the working with the wire and size of loop. You can end with a dangle (5mm crystal on a head pin)

It is a good idea to use sterling wire on this project, so that the earwires are sterling.

DOUBLE COILED WATCHBAND

This watchband is easy to make and looks great!

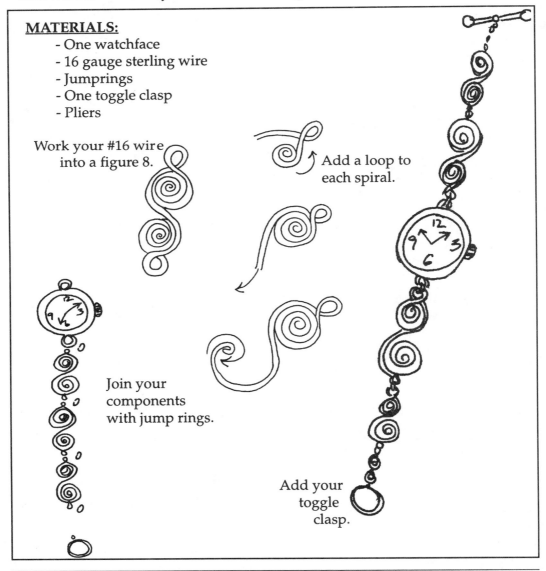

MATERIALS:
- One watchface
- 16 gauge sterling wire
- Jumprings
- One toggle clasp
- Pliers

Work your #16 wire into a figure 8.

Add a loop to each spiral.

Join your components with jump rings.

Add your toggle clasp.

This necklace uses basic linking techniques mixed with a caged, undrilled stone. By joining these units, you get an unsual necklace with lots of character.

MATERIALS:
- Nine caged crystal beads
- Ten 4mm Czech crystal bicone beads
- #22 gauge silver wire
- One large ring (from a toggle clasp)
- One hook clasp (you can make your own with #18 gauge sterling wire)
- Four jump rings (1/8")
- One larger jumpring (1/4")
- One terminated crystal (using wrapping techniques shown on page 11; wrap in the same way as the clasp shown on the end of the leather cord. The loop is for attaching.
- Pliers

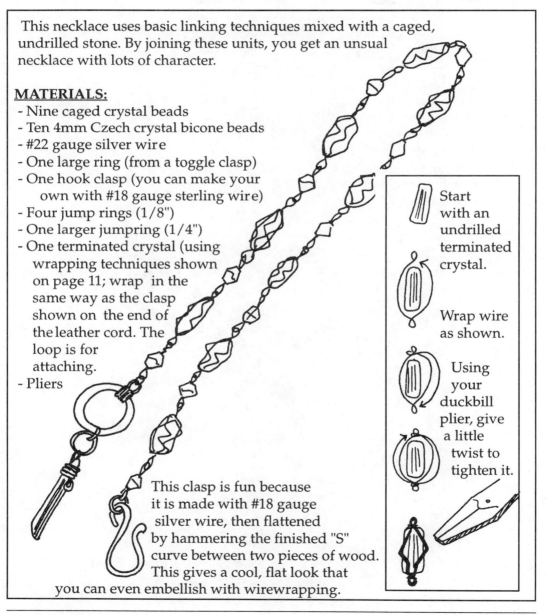

Start with an undrilled terminated crystal.

Wrap wire as shown.

Using your duckbill plier, give a little twist to tighten it.

This clasp is fun because it is made with #18 gauge silver wire, then flattened by hammering the finished "S" curve between two pieces of wood. This gives a cool, flat look that you can even embellish with wirewrapping.

Citrine and blue topaz are a beautiful combination. This bracelet is elegant and dressy enough for evening.

MATERIALS:
- Three large (20mm x 10mm) carved blue topaz beads
- Three large (20mm x 10mm) carved citrine beads
- #22 gauge wire
- Two jumprings
- Six optional jumprings
- One lobster clasp and figure 8
- Pliers

As you make your coiled ends on each side of the beads, create an exaggerated coil by continuing to wrap partially down the length of the bead.

Link the beads as you work, or you can use optional jumprings to join them. Alternate the blue topaz with the citrine.

End with your figure 8 and your lobster claw clasp.

COILED & CAGED BRACELET

The secret to this project is picking the right wire. A harder wire is more difficult to work, but it does hold its shape. Experiment to find the one that works for you.

MATERIALS:
- Marbles
- #20 gauge hard wire(you can also try #18 or #22, depending on your preferences)
- One lobster clasp and figure 8
- Jumprings   - Two or more pliers

There are two parts to this bracelet. The first part is the caged marbles. Start by making a little coil in the wire to start with (sort of like a little resting place for the marble. As you wrap the wire around the marble, it can rest in this little spot for stability.) You will pull this coil up to become the loop that links to the next bead.

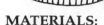

The second part is the wound beads. I found it easier to shape these beads over a glass bead, then carefully pop them out, to leave the "empty shell" of wire. Wrap your coils as closely as you can. Leave holes in the top and bottom to create a bead. You need to be careful not to disturb their shape as you do this. It's easier to use two pliers as you work.

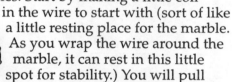

Thread these beads with eyepins to join to the next bead.

Join your segments to length with jumprings. For a variation, try using marbles of different colors, or even "fried marbles".

This is a great pin for a lapel or at the collar of a favorite blouse. Amber and silver are a beautiful combination, and this project incorporates a lot of fun techniques and embellishments.

MATERIALS:
- #20 gauge silver wire
- #24 gauge silver wire
- A mixture of amber beads
- Silver bugle beads
- Amber hearts and pi beads
- Silver "paddle" charms
- Pliers
- A wire jig

STEP ONE:

Lay out your design on your wire jig. Stagger two rows of 10 nails. Each row is offset slightly. Take a length of #18 wire, about 18 " long. Depending on how far apart you have placed your nails, you may need to adjust your length of wire. Your finished pin will end up about two inches wide. Wrap your loops as closely as possible, and work from the center of the wire. Wrap around each nail, alternating to make rounded curves. Continue on for all 20 nails. This will give you ten loops on top, and ten on the bottom.

Another way to make these loops is to work around your round nose plier. This takes a little more practice to get the loops all a uniform size.

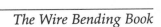

STEP TWO:

When you have completed your ten loops, make a loop that will give your pin back flexibility.

You can sharpen the end of your pinback so that it doesn't rip clothing.

STEP THREE:

To make the catch, make a loop, fold it over, and wirebend a coil to finish the look.

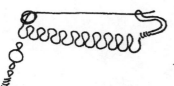

You are now ready to start adding charms.

STEP FOUR:

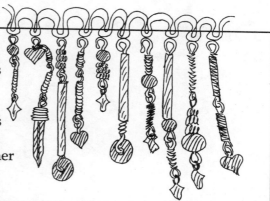

There are ten loops to fill with your treasures. Add crystals, amber hearts and beads, silver bugle beads, beads that you have coiled, little silver paddle charms, and more. This is a great way to use those odds and ends. Another alternative is to hammer your loops flat before you add your embellishments, or use twisted wire.

This is a fun pin to make. It's very modern and colorful, and you are sure to get compliments on this everytime you wear it.

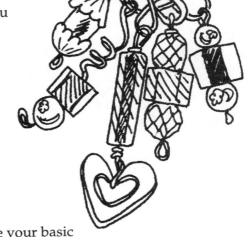

MATERIALS:
- #18 sterling wire
- An assortment of beads
- A wire jig
- Pliers

Using your jig, make your basic pin.

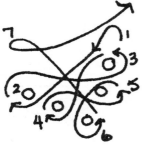

Embellish each loop with an assortment of beads.

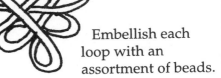

You can also make a larger pin by incorporating more loops into your pin. Place your nails at a right angle.

Wirebending is very addictive. You can make so many variations with the variety of wires available, that you will never run out of ideas.

PENDANT #1

MATERIALS

- Three feet #22 gauge sterling
    square wire
- 30 " sterling flat wire
- A stone heart about 1 1/2" wide

STEP ONE:

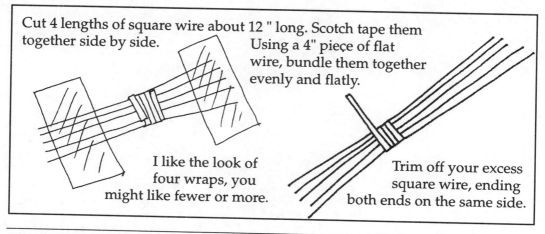

Cut 4 lengths of square wire about 12 " long. Scotch tape them together side by side. Using a 4" piece of flat wire, bundle them together evenly and flatly.

I like the look of four wraps, you might like fewer or more.

Trim off your excess square wire, ending both ends on the same side.

STEP TWO:

Pull each of the four wires out like rays.

Using your duckbill pliers, make a right angle in the outside wires.

Wrap another 4" length of flat wire to the side of each of these.

Continue on, adding one more.

STEP THREE:

Cradle the bottom of your stone in the center "basket" of wire.

Carefully pull up the sides.

Pull the center wires together, and bundle with more flat wire. Work both sides of the stone evenly.

Pull up the ends to make a collar, and wire wrap to secure.

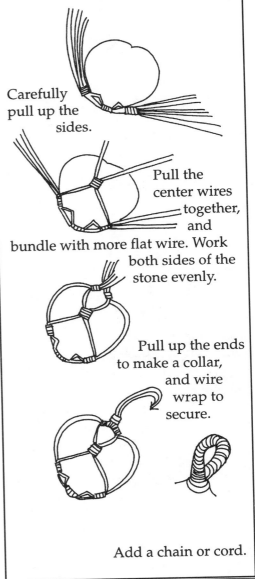

Add a chain or cord.

This pendant mixes with gold filled wire with silver wire.

PENDANT #2

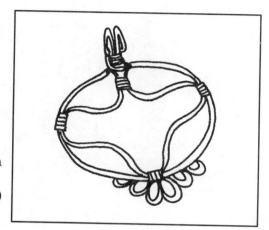

MATERIALS

- Three feet #24 gauge sterling
    square wire
- 30 " gold filled flat wire
- A cabochon about 40mmx30mm
- Duck billed plier
- Chain nose plier (2 for gripping)

STEP ONE:

Cut three one-foot lengths of sterling wire. Bundle them with 4" of gold filled wire. Pull the three strands out like a ray.

Using your pliers, Make a little curve in the two outer wires. They should be symmetrical.

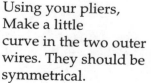

STEP TWO:

Adjust your wires around the cabochon. Wrap with the gold filled wire again on each side, and bring the ends up.

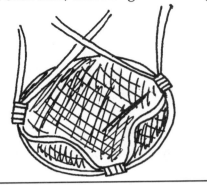

STEP THREE:

Wrap in the center front and back of the cabochon, and bring your ends up.

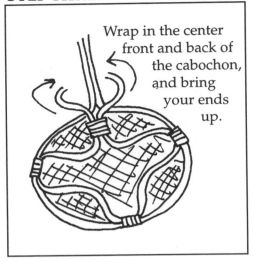

STEP FOUR:

Wrap the top, then bring your ends around to the back.

STEP FIVE:

Finish the back by wrapping up all your loose ends (literally).

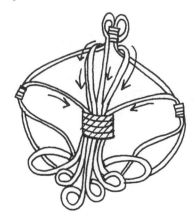

Finish with loops at the bottom. If you choose to, you can add beads to dangle.

Darice®
CREATIVE CRAFTS

Designs by: John Tistyan, Patricia Stewart & Susan M. Smith

HOLIDAY WOOD
ORNAMENTS

FACE TREE ORNAMENT SUPPLIES

- 3mm Folk Art Tree   #9171-55
- 1/2" Wood Furniture Buttons   #08638
- #3 Black Micron Pen
- 1⅝" x 3/16" Country Star   #9137-41
- 8" Thread
- 1/8" Drill Bit, Drill
- Wood Glue, Paint Brush, Blush

DELTA PAINT: Green Isle #2008   Sparkle Glaze #7012   Butter Yellow #2102

INSTRUCTIONS:

1) Paint tree and furniture buttons Green Isle. Paint star Butter Yellow.

2) Glue furniture button 2½" down from top.

3) Dot eyes Black. Draw mouth with micron pen. Blush cheeks. Dot highlights to eyes.
Refer to photo.

4) Draw lines on tree and star. Personalize star with name.

5) Paint Sparkle Glaze on tree and star.

6) Glue star to tree. Refer to photo.

7) Drill hole into top of tree. Tie thread for hanger.

RUNAWAY STAR SUPPLIES:

- Star Wood Cutout   #9171-84
- 1" Wood Circle #9147-25   2 pcs
- 1/2" Wood Heart   #9121-28
- 7/8" Wooden Country Star   #9150-73
- Furniture Button   #08640
- Glue Gun, Assorted Brushes, Gold Thread, Drill and Bit

DELTA PAINT: Opaque Yellow #2509   White #2505   Black #2506
Tomato Spice #2098   Pale Yellow #2005   Kim Gold #2602

INSTRUCTIONS:

1) Basecoat large star with Opaque Yellow, small star Pale Yellow, furniture button and
heart Tomato Spice, circles Kim Gold.

2) Dry brush cheeks with Tomato Spice. Dot eyes and center of circles, outline stars,
mouth and eyebrows with Black.

3) Dot highlights on cheeks and eyes. Stroke nose, heart and large star with White. Refer
to photo.

4) Splatter with Black and White.

5) Drill hole for hanger at top and tie gold thread to hanger.

RING

You can make beautiful rings with found stones, seashells, or whatever undrilled treasures you have.

MATERIALS:

- Five feet #24 gauge sterling wire (this amount may vary by your wrapping technique
- One large stone (this is a glass cabochon)
- Pliers

STEP ONE:

Bundle 4 one-foot lengths of wire in three places. You'll be using all one type of wire for this.

STEP TWO:

Curve these wires into a circle. Use the ring sizer on page 17 as a guide.

Pull out one wireon each side. Intertwine the other wires, and let these two form a "basket" for your stone.

STEP THREE:

Rest your stone on the two wires. Twist to secure.

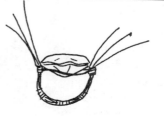

Crisscross your remaining wires over the stone to hold it in place. Twist and secure.
Curl the ends of the wire with your round nose pliers. Finish your ends smoothly.

"OCTOPUS" PIN

MATERIALS

- Ten feet #20 gauge silver wire
- 10" silver 1/8" wide flat wire
- A cabochon
- Round nose plier
- Chain nose plier (2 for gripping)

STEP ONE:

Cut nine one-foot lengths of wire. Bundle them securely with six turns of your flat wire.

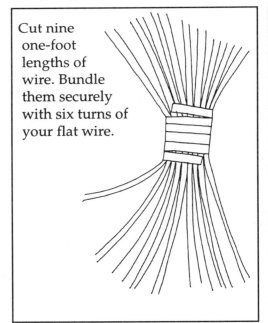

STEP TWO:

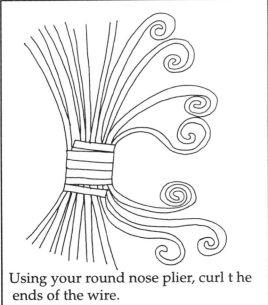

Using your round nose plier, curl the ends of the wire.

STEP THREE:

Continue bending the tendrils until all nine arms have curled ends.

STEP FOUR:

Add your pinback by wrapping wire around the end tendrils and shaping.

STEP FIVE:

Glue a cabochon onto the front of your flat wire.

You can also embellish by adding dangles to each of the curls.

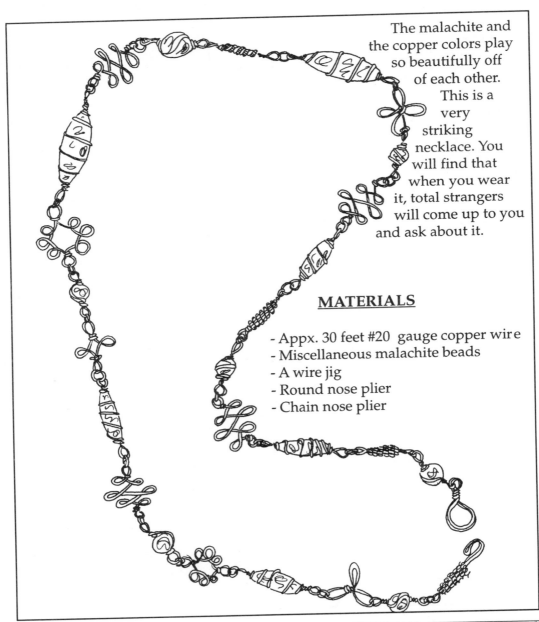

The malachite and the copper colors play so beautifully off of each other. This is a very striking necklace. You will find that when you wear it, total strangers will come up to you and ask about it.

MATERIALS

- Appx. 30 feet #20 gauge copper wire
- Miscellaneous malachite beads
- A wire jig
- Round nose plier
- Chain nose plier

The secret to this necklace are the repeated   links that are made by using the wire jig. The dots above show the configuration of the nails. All of the designs on the right were made by wrapping wire around the nails.

The malachite beads were wrapped with copper wire.

Wound beads were made and added into the design.

The clasp was made by using the same technique and adding a hook.

The matching eye was made from a double loop of wire.

Many projects can be made by simply repeating the same wirebend over and over. That's why jigs are so helpful for making uniform components.

There are certain shapes that seem to be classic. If you look at jewelry designed or influenced by Pablo Picasso, Mondrian and Alexander Calder, you will see many repeatable patterns.

The "W" is great for chokers, belts, bracelets and watchbands.

It entails making exactly the same shape over and over.

A variation is to twist the center loop sideways at a right angle, to make a perpendicular connection.

You can also vary the proportions of the loops.

The "V" shape is another popular classic.

By using jumprings and various attachments, you can create combinations that are fun and different.

Knitting with wire is a bit of a challenge when you first attempt it. You will find, however, that once you try it, it's quite addictive. Projects work up fast and very strong.

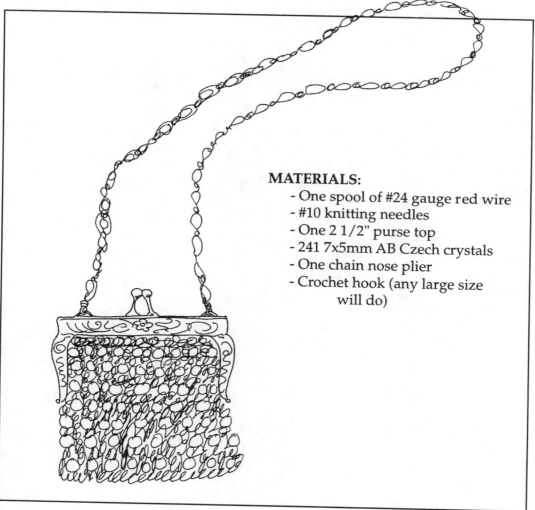

MATERIALS:
- One spool of #24 gauge red wire
- #10 knitting needles
- One 2 1/2" purse top
- 241 7x5mm AB Czech crystals
- One chain nose plier
- Crochet hook (any large size will do)

STEP ONE:

Thread 198 crystal onto the red wire.

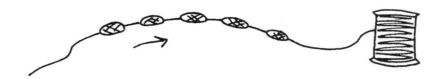

Rewind the wire back onto the spool with the beads on it.

STEP TWO:

Cast 13 stitches onto your knitting needles. You'll be working in the stockinette stitch. The end two stitches on each side do not get beads, however, be sure to slip a bead onto each stitch of the center 9 stitches as you work.

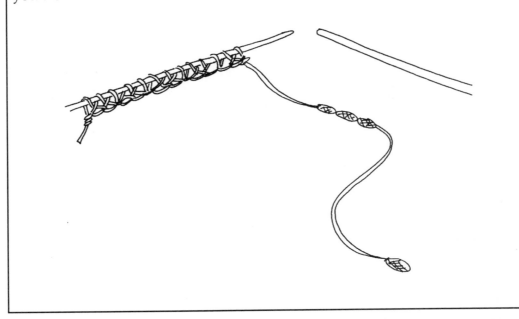

STEP THREE:

Continue on for 22 rows.

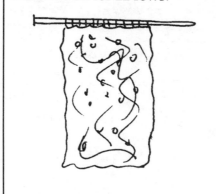

STEP FOUR:

Carefully bind off your stitches.

Secure the last one so that the stitches don't pull out.

STEP FIVE:

Fold the purse in half. Taking a separate piece of wire, "stitch" up each side of the purse.

Attach to the purse frame by weaving a piece of wire in and out of the holes in the purse top and the loops of the knitted piece.

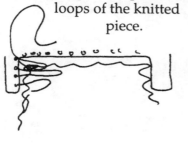

STEP SIX:

TO MAKE THE STRAP:
Add 43 beads to the spool of wire. Make a loop to attach the end to the purse top. Single crochet, with a crystal in each stitch, and connect the second side.

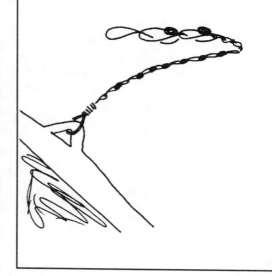

A PEARL WRAPPING VARIATION

Wrap pearls with a "figure 8" weave to give a textured look. Use #32 wire.

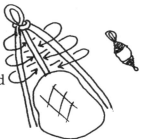

EASY ARMBAND

Bend and hammer #14 or #16 sterling wire.

FIGURE "8" EARRINGS

Make two "S" curves. If you overlap them, they become a figure 8 with movement.

LOOPED CHOKER VARIATION

Use wire and chain to add loops to your necklaces.

DAISY EARRINGS

Wirebend and hammer these flat

HAT PINS

sharpen the ends with needle files.

add charms and dangles.

Wendy Simpson Conner is no stranger to beads. As a third-generation bead artist, she grew up with beads from a very early age. Her grandmother was the jewelry and costume designer for the Ziegfeld Follies.

Being from a creative family, Wendy spent her childhood doing many types of crafts in a rural community. ("There just wasn't anything else to do!"). Over the years, she has mastered many techniques, but beads have remained her first love.

She worked as a designer in television for awhile, and also has a strong illustration background (she always insists on doing her own illustrations).

Wendy has been teaching vocational beadwork classes for San Diego Community Colleges and the Grossmont Adult School District for fifteen years. She not only teaches beading technique, but also the dynamics of running your own jewelry business.

Her first book, *The Best Little Beading Book,* was the result of many of her classroom handouts. All of her books, including *The Beaded Lampshade Book, The Magical Beaded Medicine Bag Book, The "Knotty" Macrame and Beading Book, The Beaded Watchband Book , The Chain & Crystal Book, The Beaded Jewelry for a Wedding Book, The Children's Beading Book,* and *The Cat Lover's Beaded Project Book,* have been very popular. They are part of **The Beading Books Series,** a collection of 25 books devoted to preserving beading techniques and history. Many of these books are also available in kit form. These kits include the original book, plus materials for making the projects shown.

Wendy designs jewelry for several television shows, as well as the celebrities on them.

Recently, she produced, wrote and directed *The Bead Movement,* the critically acclaimed one hour documentary which examines the world's fascination with beads. This is now also available in a 27 minute director's cut.

Wendy is available to teach workshops. If you are interested, please contact her through the Interstellar Publishing Company, Post Office Box 2215, La Mesa, California, 91943.

INTERSTELLAR

TRADING & PUBLISHING COMPANY

Other Books, Kits, and Videos By the
Interstellar Trading & Publishing Company:

The Best Little Beading Book

The Beaded Lampshade Book

The Magical Beaded Medicine Bag Book

The "Knotty" Macrame & Beading Book

The Beaded Watchband Book

The Chain & Crystal Book

The Beaded Jewelry for a Wedding Book

The Children's Beading Book

The Cat Lover's Beaded Project Book

The Wirebending Book

The Beading On Fabric Book

The "Knotty" Macrame Kit

The Beaded Watchband Kit

The Magical Beaded Medicine Bag Kit

The Children's Beading Kit

"The Bead Movement", a one hour documentary about beads

"The Bead Movement/Director's Cut" (27 min.)

If you would like a list of other titles and forthcoming books from the Interstellar Trading & Publishing Company, please send a stamped, self-addressed envelope to:

**THE INTERSTELLAR TRADING & PUBLISHING COMPANY
POST OFFICE BOX 2215
LA MESA, CALIFORNIA, 91943**